Words At Work
Vol. I

Carol L Rickard, LCSW

Well YOUniversity® Publications

www.WellYOUniversity.com

Copyright © 2013 Carol L Rickard & Well YOUniversity Publications

All Rights Reserved. No part of this book may be reproduced for resale, redistribution, or any other purposes (including but not limited to eBooks, pamphlets, articles, video, & handouts or slides for lectures or workshops) Permission to reproduce these materials for those and any other purposes must be obtained in writing from the author. Licensing is available for commercial use.

ISBN-13: 978-0-9821010-6-3

DEDICATION

This book is dedicated to all the patients I have had the privilege of working with.

CONTENTS

Acknowledgments

1	Acceptance	27	Toxic
2	Addiction	28	Truth
3	Ask	29	Worries
4	Attitude	30	Adapt
5	Blame	31	React
6	Change	32	Purpose
7	Choice	33	Parents
8	Fear	34	Risk
9	Education	35	Life
10	Fact	36	Purpose
11	Faith	37	Finish
12	Feel	38	Cope
13	Forgive	39	Cravings
14	Focus	40	Consistent
15	Goal	41	Healing
16	Excuse	42	Imagine
17	Gratitude	43	Past
18	Habit	44	Calm
19	Hate	45	Serve
20	Hope	46	Anger
21	Let Go	47	Complain
22	Now	48	Discipline
23	Present	49	Doubt
24	Promise	50	Dream
25	Sober	51	Meditation
26	Substitution	52	Mindful

ACKNOWLEDGMENTS

I would like to say that none of this would have been possible without your love and support. Thank you for believing in me and always giving me the encouragement to pursue my dreams.

© 2013 WELL YOUNIVERSITY PUBLICATIONS – Licensing Available

ACCEPTANCE

A

CONSCIOUS

CHOICE

ENABLING

PEOPLE

TO

ACKNOWLEDGE

NEW

CIRCUMSTANCES

EXIST

© 2013 WELL YOUNIVERSITY PUBLICATIONS – Licensing Available

A

DEADLY

DISEASE

INFLICTING

CONTINUOUS

TRAUMA

IN

OUR

NEIGHBORHOODS

© 2013 WELL YOUNIVERISTY PUBLICATIONS – Licensing Available

ACQUIRE

SELF

KNOWLEDGE

FAILURE

FINDING
AN
IMPORTANT
LESSON
USING
REAL
EXPERIENCES

Become
Lost
Amongst
Many
Excuses

© 2013 WELL YOUNIVERSITY PUBLICATIONS – Licensing Available

CHANGE

CREATING
HEALTHY
AND
NEW
GROWTH
EXPERIENCES

© 2013 WELL YOUNIVERSITY PUBLICATIONS – Licensing Available

© 2013 WELL YOUNIVERISTY PUBLICATIONS – Licensing Available

CONTROLLING
HOW
OUR
INTENTIONS
CREATE
EXPERIENCES

© 2013 WELL YOUNIVERSITY PUBLICATIONS – Licensing Available

Find

Emotion

Alters

Reality

© 2013 WELL YOUNIVERISTY PUBLICATIONS – Licensing Available

EACH
DAY
UNDERSTANDING
COMES
ALONG
TO
IMPROVE
OUR
NATURE

FACE
A
CONCRETE
TRUTH

Find
An
Internal
Trusting
Hold

FULLY
EXAMINE
EMOTIONAL
LESSONS

© 2013 WELL YOUNIVERISTY PUBLICATIONS – Licensing Available

FIND
OURSELVES
RELEASING
GRIEVANCES
INCLUDING
VICTIM
EXPERIENCES

© 2013 WELL YOUNIVERSITY PUBLICATIONS – Licensing Available

FIX

OUR

CONCENTRATION

UNTIL

SUCCESSFUL

Get
Our
Activity
Lined-Up

© 2013 WELL YOUNIVERSITY PUBLICATIONS – Licensing Available

ENGAGE

XTERNAL

CIRCUMSTANCES

UNDERMINING

SELF

EMPOWERMENT

© 2013 WELL YOUNIVERISTY PUBLICATIONS – Licensing Available

GIVE
RESPECT
AND
THANKS
INTO
THE
USUAL
DAILY
EXPERIENCES

HABIT

HAVING

A

BEHAVIOR

INTERNALLY

TRIGGERED

HOLDING

A

TOXIC

EMOTION

HOLDING

ONTO

POSITIVE

EXPECTATIONS

Leave
Everything
To

God's
Ownership

NOTICE

ONLY

WHAT-IS

© 2013 WELL YOUNIVERISTY PUBLICATIONS – Licensing Available

PURPOSELY

RECOGNIZE

EVERY

SINGLE

EXPERIENCE

NOW

TAKING-PLACE

© 2013 WELL YOUNIVERSITY PUBLICATIONS – Licensing Available

PROMISE

PLACE

RESPONSIBILITY

ON

MAKING

INTENTIONS

STAY

EXECUTED

STOP
OLD
BEHAVIORS
EMBRACING
RECOVERY

SWITCHING
UNHEALTHY
BEHAVIORS
SIMPLY
TAKING
INTENTION
TO
USE &
TRANSFERRING
INTO
OTHER
NEGATIVES

TAKE-AWAY

OUR

XISTENCE

INSTEAD

CONTRIBUTING

TAKE

RESPONSIBILITY

UNTIL

TOTALLY

HONEST

© 2013 WELL YOUNIVERISTY PUBLICATIONS – Licensing Available

Waste
Our
Ready
Resources
Instead
Examining
Strengths

ADAPT

A

DELIBERATE

ADJUSTMENT

PRODUCING

TRANSFORMATION

RELEASE

EMOTION

AND

CREATE

TROUBLE

POWERFUL

UNDERLYING

REASON

PUSHING

OURSELVES

SERVE

EVERYDAY

© 2013 WELL YOUNIVERISTY PUBLICATIONS – Licensing Available

PROVIDE

A

RESPONSIBLE

ENVIRONMENT

NEEDED

TO

SUCCEED

RESULT
IS
SELDOM
KNOWN

© 2013 WELL YOUNIVERISTY PUBLICATIONS – Licensing Available

Living

Intentionally &

Fully

Engaged

© 2013 WELL YOUNIVERSITY PUBLICATIONS – Licensing Available

PURPOSE

POWERFUL

UNDERLYING

REASON

PUSHING

OURSELVES

STRETCH

EVERYDAY

Focus
In
Now
Instead
Stopping
Halfway

© 2013 WELL YOUNIVERSITY PUBLICATIONS – Licensing Available

CHALLENGE

OUR

PROBLEMS

EFFECTIVELY

CONSTANT
REMINDERS
ACTING
VERY
INFLUENTIAL
NEEDING
GREAT
SUPERVISION

CONCENTRATE
ON
NOT
STOPPING
INSTEAD
STRENGTHEN
THE
EFFORT
NEEDED
TODAY

© 2013 WELL YOUNIVERISTY PUBLICATIONS – Licensing Available

HOLD
EMOTION
AND
LETTING
IT
NATURALLY
GO.

© 2013 WELL YOUNIVERSITY PUBLICATIONS – Licensing Available

Incredible
Mental
Activity
Generating
Ideas
Not
Existing

POWERFUL

ALIGNMENT

SABOTAGING

TODAY

C REATE
A
L EVEL
M INDSET

See

Everyone

Receives

Valuable

Experience

ANGER

NATURALLY
GENERATED
EMOTIONAL
RESPONSE

CONCENTRATE

ON

O

MAKING

PROBLEMS

LARGER

ACTUALLY

INCREASING

NEGATIVITY

© 2013 WELL YOUNIVERSITY PUBLICATIONS – Licensing Available

DECIDING
I
STAY
COMMITTED
IN
PURPOSE
LETTING
IN
NO
EXCUSE

DOUBT

DWELL

ON

UNFOUNDED

BELIEFS &

THOUGHTS

© 2013 WELL YOUNIVERSITY PUBLICATIONS – Licensing Available

DARINGLY
RECOGNIZE
EXPERIENCES
AS
MINE

Mind
Exercises
Developing &
Increasing
The
Ability
To
Improve
Our
Nature

© 2013 WELL YOUNIVERSITY PUBLICATIONS – Licensing Available

Moments

Intentionally

Noticed

Directly

Fixing

Unconscious

Living

© 2013 WELL YOUNIVERISTY PUBLICATIONS – Licensing Available

ABOUT THE AUTHOR

Carol Rickard, LCSW, is a nationally recognized stress and wellness expert. She is the founder of Well YOUniversity, a health education company and author of several self health books including LifeTools, Putting Your Weight Loss on Auto, Emotional Eating, & Moving Beyond Depression. She is creator of the L.I.F.E. Recovery & Wellness Program, recently recognized by The Joint Commission (TJC)as a "leading practice". For information regarding wellness resources, training programs and workshops, please visit www.WellYOUniversity.com or email her at Carol@WellYOUniversity.com

OTHER BOOKS BY CAROL L. RICKARD, LCSW

Moving Beyond Depression: A Step by Step System for Reclaiming Your Life From Depression

Emotional Eating: How to STOP Using Food to Cope

LifeTools: How to Manage Life INSTEAD OF Life Managing You!

Putting Your Weight Loss on Auto: 7 Laws a Car Can Teach You About Lasting Weight Loss

Creating Compliance: A Toolbox of Coping Skills Handouts & Activities to Foster Treatment Compliance

Relapse Prevention: Reproducible Exercises for Relapse Prevention in Mental Health

www.ingramcontent.com/pod-product-compliance
Lightning Source LLC
LaVergne TN
LVHW061344060426
835512LV00016B/2655